PRINCEWILL LAGANG

Entrepreneurship in Healthcare: Innovations for Better Lives

First published by PRINCEWILL LAGANG 2023

Copyright © 2023 by Princewill Lagang

All rights reserved. No part of this publication may be reproduced, stored or transmitted in any form or by any means, electronic, mechanical, photocopying, recording, scanning, or otherwise without written permission from the publisher. It is illegal to copy this book, post it to a website, or distribute it by any other means without permission.

Princewill Lagang asserts the moral right to be identified as the author of this work.

First edition

This book was professionally typeset on Reedsy.
Find out more at reedsy.com

Contents

1. Entrepreneurship in Healthcare: Innovations for Better Lives — 1
2. Technological Advancements in Healthcare Entrepreneurship — 5
3. Biotechnology and Healthcare Entrepreneurship — 9
4. Social Entrepreneurship in Healthcare — 12
5. Global Healthcare Entrepreneurship and Impact — 15
6. Healthcare Entrepreneurship in the Digital Age — 18
7. Healthcare Entrepreneurship and Ethical Considerations — 21
8. Financing Healthcare Entrepreneurship — 24
9. Scaling Healthcare Entrepreneurship — 28
10. Healthcare Entrepreneurship and Future Trends — 31
11. Healthcare Entrepreneurship and Resilience — 34
12. Healthcare Entrepreneurship and Social Responsibility — 37
13. Summary — 40

1

Entrepreneurship in Healthcare: Innovations for Better Lives

Introduction

Healthcare is a fundamental aspect of human well-being, and it plays a pivotal role in shaping the quality of our lives. Over the years, healthcare has evolved significantly, driven by scientific advancements, technological breakthroughs, and entrepreneurial spirit. In this first chapter, we delve into the world of entrepreneurship in healthcare and how it has been a driving force for positive change and innovation in the field. We will explore the unique challenges and opportunities faced by healthcare entrepreneurs and the impact of their endeavors on the lives of individuals and communities.

Section 1: The State of Healthcare

1.1 The Importance of Healthcare

Healthcare is a cornerstone of any thriving society. It encompasses a wide range of services, from prevention and diagnosis to treatment and rehabilitation, all aimed at improving the health and well-being of individuals and populations. It affects our ability to lead fulfilling lives, contributes to economic productivity, and has a profound impact on public health. As healthcare needs grow and change, it presents both challenges and opportunities for entrepreneurs to make a difference.

1.2 The Current Landscape

The healthcare landscape is characterized by an increasing demand for services due to a growing and aging population, the rise of chronic diseases, and the high cost of medical care. Access to quality healthcare varies widely, with disparities in affordability and availability, often leaving underserved communities at a disadvantage. Entrepreneurs have recognized these challenges and are pioneering innovative solutions to address them.

Section 2: The Role of Entrepreneurship

2.1 Entrepreneurship in Healthcare

Entrepreneurship in healthcare involves identifying unmet needs, developing creative solutions, and implementing them to create value for patients, healthcare providers, and the industry as a whole. Entrepreneurs in this field range from medical professionals, researchers, and engineers to business-savvy individuals who see an opportunity to make a positive impact. These entrepreneurs play a crucial role in driving progress and transforming the healthcare sector.

2.2 Key Drivers of Entrepreneurship

Several factors drive entrepreneurship in healthcare:

a. Technological Advancements: The rapid pace of technological innovation, including artificial intelligence, telemedicine, and wearable devices, has opened up new possibilities for healthcare entrepreneurs.

b. Regulatory Changes: Evolving regulations and policies, such as telehealth reimbursement and data privacy laws, create opportunities for innovative business models.

c. Market Demand: The increasing demand for personalized and convenient healthcare services has led to the emergence of niche markets and entrepreneurial ventures.

d. Funding Opportunities: Venture capital, grants, and government incentives are readily available to support healthcare startups.

Section 3: Challenges in Healthcare Entrepreneurship

3.1 Regulatory Hurdles

Navigating the complex regulatory environment in healthcare can be a significant challenge for entrepreneurs. Compliance with laws related to healthcare standards, privacy, and reimbursement is essential but can be daunting.

3.2 Clinical Validation

Developing and proving the effectiveness of healthcare innovations often requires rigorous clinical trials and studies. These can be time-consuming and costly, posing a barrier for some startups.

3.3 Reimbursement Models

Understanding and integrating various reimbursement models, such as insurance, government programs, and out-of-pocket payments, is crucial for the success of healthcare ventures.

Section 4: Success Stories

4.1 Case Study: Telemedicine Revolution

Explore the meteoric rise of telemedicine as a prime example of healthcare entrepreneurship. Understand how it has improved accessibility and quality of care while highlighting the role of innovative startups in the telehealth ecosystem.

4.2 Case Study: Genomic Sequencing

Delve into the world of genomic sequencing and precision medicine, demonstrating how entrepreneurs have harnessed the power of genetics to develop personalized treatment plans and diagnostics.

Conclusion

This chapter has provided an overview of the dynamic landscape of healthcare entrepreneurship, emphasizing its critical role in addressing the evolving needs of the healthcare sector and society at large. As we move forward, it is essential to explore the innovative solutions and remarkable stories of entrepreneurs who are working tirelessly to make healthcare more accessible, affordable, and effective. In the subsequent chapters, we will delve deeper into specific areas of healthcare entrepreneurship, including technological advancements, biotechnology, and social entrepreneurship in healthcare, to gain a comprehensive understanding of the field and its impact on bettering lives.

2

Technological Advancements in Healthcare Entrepreneurship

Introduction

In the ever-evolving landscape of healthcare, technological advancements have played a pivotal role in driving innovation and improving patient care. This chapter delves into the intersection of technology and healthcare entrepreneurship, exploring the various ways in which cutting-edge innovations have transformed the industry. From telemedicine to wearable devices and artificial intelligence applications, we will examine how entrepreneurs have harnessed the power of technology to revolutionize healthcare for the better.

Section 1: Telemedicine and Remote Care

1.1 Telehealth's Rise

Telemedicine, once considered a niche area of healthcare, has gained widespread acceptance and prominence in recent years. This section will explore the factors contributing to its surge, such as the COVID-19 pandemic, and the entrepreneurial ventures that have leveraged telehealth to expand access to care.

1.2 Telemedicine Platforms

We will examine the various telehealth platforms and apps that have emerged, connecting patients with healthcare providers remotely. Case studies will illustrate how telemedicine startups have disrupted traditional healthcare delivery models, offering convenient and cost-effective care options.

Section 2: Wearable Health Technology

2.1 The Wearable Revolution

Wearable health technology, including fitness trackers, smartwatches, and health-monitoring devices, has transformed how individuals engage with their health. This section will discuss the role of entrepreneurs in driving the development and adoption of these technologies.

2.2 Remote Patient Monitoring

Entrepreneurs have capitalized on the potential of wearable devices to provide continuous health monitoring, enabling early detection of health issues and facilitating more personalized care. We'll explore examples of startups that have excelled in this field.

Section 3: Artificial Intelligence in Healthcare

3.1 AI's Impact

Artificial intelligence (AI) is a game-changer in healthcare, with applications ranging from diagnostics and treatment recommendations to streamlining administrative processes. This section will investigate the profound impact of AI on healthcare and the entrepreneurial endeavors driving this change.

3.2 Diagnostic AI

Entrepreneurs have developed AI-powered diagnostic tools that can analyze medical images, lab results, and patient data with unparalleled accuracy. Case studies will highlight how these innovations are improving diagnostic speed and accuracy.

Section 4: Personalized Medicine and Genomic Sequencing

4.1 Genomic Medicine

Genomic sequencing has ushered in an era of personalized medicine, where treatment plans are tailored to an individual's genetic makeup. This section will delve into the entrepreneurial efforts that have brought genomic sequencing to the forefront of healthcare.

4.2 Startups in Genomic Sequencing

We will explore how startups in the field of genomic sequencing have made this technology more accessible and affordable, revolutionizing disease prevention, diagnosis, and treatment.

Conclusion

Chapter 2 has shed light on the transformative impact of technological advancements on healthcare entrepreneurship. From telemedicine to wearable technology, artificial intelligence, and genomic sequencing, entrepreneurs have harnessed cutting-edge technologies to improve healthcare delivery, enhance patient outcomes, and drive efficiency in the industry. The subsequent chapters will continue to explore other facets of healthcare entrepreneurship, revealing how these innovations are not only shaping the future of healthcare but also improving the quality of lives across the globe.

3

Biotechnology and Healthcare Entrepreneurship

Introduction

Biotechnology has long been a driving force in healthcare, enabling breakthroughs in drug development, diagnostics, and therapeutic interventions. In this chapter, we delve into the realm of biotechnology and its role in healthcare entrepreneurship. We explore how entrepreneurs are leveraging advancements in biotech to create innovative solutions for complex medical challenges, from precision medicine to gene therapies, and how they navigate the unique challenges of this field.

Section 1: Precision Medicine

1.1 The Promise of Precision Medicine

Precision medicine aims to tailor medical treatments to the individual characteristics of each patient, taking into account their genetic makeup, environment, and lifestyle. This section introduces the concept of precision medicine and its potential to revolutionize healthcare.

1.2 Genomic Profiling

Entrepreneurs in biotechnology have played a crucial role in making genomic profiling and personalized treatment plans more accessible. We'll examine the entrepreneurs and startups driving this field forward.

Section 2: Cell and Gene Therapies

2.1 Cutting-Edge Therapies

Cell and gene therapies represent groundbreaking approaches to treat a variety of diseases, including genetic disorders and certain cancers. This section explores the potential of these therapies and the pioneering work of healthcare entrepreneurs.

2.2 Commercializing Cell and Gene Therapies

Bringing cell and gene therapies to market requires overcoming unique regulatory and logistical challenges. We'll discuss the entrepreneurial efforts involved in commercializing these innovative treatments.

Section 3: Drug Discovery and Development

3.1 Drug Development Process

Drug discovery and development are complex, lengthy, and expensive processes. Entrepreneurs are finding innovative ways to streamline and accelerate these processes using biotechnology, artificial intelligence, and data analytics.

3.2 Biotech Startups in Drug Development

Case studies will illustrate how biotechnology startups are changing the landscape of drug discovery, with a focus on rare diseases, oncology, and other areas of high unmet medical need.

Section 4: The Challenges of Biotechnology Entrepreneurship

4.1 Regulatory and Ethical Considerations

Navigating the regulatory landscape for biotechnology products is a formidable challenge. Entrepreneurs in this field must also consider ethical issues related to gene editing, human trials, and the potential misuse of biotech advances.

4.2 Funding and Market Dynamics

Biotechnology startups often require substantial capital and face unique market dynamics. We will explore how entrepreneurs secure funding and make strategic decisions to navigate these challenges.

Conclusion

Chapter 3 has illuminated the profound impact of biotechnology on healthcare entrepreneurship. Entrepreneurs in this field are at the forefront of revolutionizing healthcare through precision medicine, cell and gene therapies, and drug development. Despite the regulatory complexities and ethical considerations, their innovative solutions have the potential to transform the lives of patients and reshape the future of healthcare. In the upcoming chapters, we will continue to explore the diverse and dynamic landscape of healthcare entrepreneurship, uncovering how entrepreneurs are shaping the industry and contributing to better lives.

4

Social Entrepreneurship in Healthcare

Introduction

While healthcare entrepreneurship often focuses on technological advancements and biotechnological innovations, there is a growing recognition of the role of social entrepreneurship in addressing systemic healthcare challenges. In this chapter, we explore how social entrepreneurs are making a significant impact on healthcare access, equity, and sustainability. These individuals and organizations are driven by a mission to create positive social and health outcomes, often in underserved communities and resource-constrained environments.

Section 1: The Social Determinants of Health

1.1 Understanding Social Determinants

Social determinants of health, such as education, socioeconomic status, and access to healthcare, play a critical role in shaping individual health outcomes. We will explore the profound impact of these factors on healthcare disparities and the need for innovative solutions.

1.2 Social Entrepreneurship's Focus

Social entrepreneurs in healthcare are dedicated to addressing these determinants by creating solutions that go beyond medical treatments and focus on improving the overall well-being of communities.

Section 2: Access to Care

2.1 Addressing Healthcare Deserts

Many communities lack access to basic healthcare services, leading to disparities in health outcomes. Social entrepreneurs are working to bridge this gap by establishing community health clinics, mobile health units, and telehealth initiatives.

2.2 Case Studies: Access Initiatives

We will examine successful examples of social entrepreneurial ventures that have expanded access to care, providing insights into their strategies and impact.

Section 3: Health Equity

3.1 Racial and Ethnic Disparities

Racial and ethnic disparities in healthcare outcomes persist and continue to be a pressing issue. Social entrepreneurs are actively engaged in efforts to eliminate these inequities and ensure that healthcare is accessible to all.

3.2 Maternal and Child Health

Maternal and child health disparities are a significant concern. We will explore how social entrepreneurs are addressing these disparities through initiatives such as community health education, prenatal care, and support for new mothers.

Section 4: Sustainability and Social Impact

4.1 Environmental Impact

The healthcare sector has a significant environmental footprint. Social entrepreneurs are driving sustainable healthcare practices through initiatives that reduce waste, energy consumption, and environmental impact.

4.2 Measuring Social Impact

We will discuss methods for assessing and quantifying the social impact of healthcare entrepreneurship, as well as the importance of accountability and transparency.

Conclusion

Chapter 4 has highlighted the vital role of social entrepreneurship in healthcare, addressing healthcare access, equity, and sustainability. Social entrepreneurs are creating innovative solutions to tackle the social determinants of health and promote better lives in underserved and marginalized communities. Their work not only improves health outcomes but also contributes to a more just and equitable healthcare system. In the subsequent chapters, we will continue to explore various facets of healthcare entrepreneurship, shedding light on the multifaceted ways in which entrepreneurs are shaping the future of healthcare for the benefit of individuals and communities.

5

Global Healthcare Entrepreneurship and Impact

Introduction

Healthcare entrepreneurship is not limited to a single region or country. Entrepreneurs worldwide are contributing to the betterment of healthcare systems, creating innovative solutions, and addressing global health challenges. This chapter explores the international landscape of healthcare entrepreneurship, highlighting the impact of cross-border collaboration, global health initiatives, and the unique challenges faced by entrepreneurs operating on a global scale.

Section 1: Cross-Border Collaboration

1.1 Collaborative Partnerships

Collaboration between healthcare entrepreneurs, organizations, and governments across borders is essential in addressing global health challenges. We will explore how international partnerships can lead to the development of innovative solutions and the sharing of best practices.

1.2 Telemedicine and Telehealth Across Borders

The global reach of telemedicine and telehealth solutions will be examined, showcasing examples of cross-border telemedicine initiatives that connect patients with healthcare providers from around the world.

Section 2: Global Health Initiatives

2.1 International Aid and Relief

Non-governmental organizations and social entrepreneurs play a critical role in providing healthcare assistance and relief in regions affected by crises, including natural disasters and conflicts.

2.2 Case Studies: Global Health Organizations

We will discuss case studies of global health organizations and initiatives that have successfully improved healthcare access, disease prevention, and health education in underserved regions.

Section 3: Emerging Markets and Global Expansion

3.1 Emerging Market Opportunities

Emerging markets present unique opportunities for healthcare entrepreneurs, with untapped potential for innovative solutions, cost-effective care, and improved healthcare infrastructure.

3.2 Challenges in Global Expansion

Expanding healthcare entrepreneurship globally is not without its challenges, including regulatory complexities, cultural differences, and the need for adaptability.

Section 4: Pandemic Preparedness and Response

4.1 Lessons from Global Crises

The COVID-19 pandemic serves as a stark reminder of the importance of global preparedness and response to healthcare crises. We will examine how healthcare entrepreneurs and organizations have contributed to pandemic response efforts.

4.2 Innovations in Vaccine Distribution

The rapid development and distribution of COVID-19 vaccines have been a global effort. This section will showcase entrepreneurial initiatives in vaccine development and distribution, highlighting their global impact.

Conclusion

Chapter 5 has provided an overview of the global landscape of healthcare entrepreneurship, emphasizing the importance of cross-border collaboration, global health initiatives, and the opportunities and challenges of expanding healthcare solutions on a global scale. Entrepreneurs in healthcare are not bound by national borders; their impact extends across continents, improving the lives of people worldwide. In the upcoming chapters, we will continue to explore the multifaceted and ever-evolving world of healthcare entrepreneurship, showcasing the diverse ways in which entrepreneurs are shaping the future of healthcare on a global scale.

6

Healthcare Entrepreneurship in the Digital Age

Introduction

The digital age has ushered in a new era of healthcare entrepreneurship, marked by the convergence of technology, data, and patient-centric care. In this chapter, we explore the profound impact of digital innovations on healthcare, from electronic health records (EHRs) to telemedicine and artificial intelligence. We will examine how entrepreneurs are leveraging the power of the digital age to improve patient experiences, optimize healthcare operations, and drive transformative change in the industry.

Section 1: Electronic Health Records (EHRs) and Health Information Technology

1.1 The Evolution of EHRs

Electronic Health Records have revolutionized healthcare by digitizing patient information, enabling interoperability, and facilitating data-driven decision-making. We will delve into the development of EHR systems and their role in healthcare entrepreneurship.

1.2 Startups in Health Information Technology

Entrepreneurs are driving innovation in Health Information Technology (HIT) by developing EHR systems, health data analytics platforms, and patient engagement tools. We will explore the work of these startups and their impact on healthcare delivery.

Section 2: Telemedicine and Virtual Care

2.1 Telehealth's Digital Transformation

Telemedicine has evolved with digital technology, providing patients with convenient, remote access to healthcare services. This section explores the digital platforms and mobile apps that have shaped telehealth.

2.2 The Digital Patient Experience

Entrepreneurs have created virtual care solutions that enhance the patient experience through video consultations, remote monitoring, and secure communication. Case studies will highlight innovative startups in telehealth.

Section 3: Artificial Intelligence and Healthcare Analytics

3.1 AI in Healthcare

Artificial intelligence is transforming healthcare by improving diagnostics, treatment recommendations, and predictive analytics. We will explore the impact of AI on healthcare entrepreneurship.

3.2 Data-Driven Decision-Making

Entrepreneurs in healthcare are harnessing the power of big data and healthcare analytics to optimize clinical and operational processes. We'll showcase examples of AI-driven startups that are making a difference.

Section 4: Patient-Centric and Digital Health

4.1 Patient Empowerment

Digital health solutions empower patients to take control of their health through mobile apps, wearables, and patient portals. We will discuss how entrepreneurs are driving patient-centric care.

4.2 Remote Monitoring and Chronic Disease Management

Entrepreneurs have developed digital tools that enable remote monitoring and management of chronic conditions, improving patient outcomes and reducing healthcare costs.

Conclusion

Chapter 6 has illuminated the transformative impact of the digital age on healthcare entrepreneurship. The convergence of digital health, EHRs, telemedicine, and AI has reshaped the industry, making healthcare more accessible, efficient, and patient-centered. In the upcoming chapters, we will continue to explore the dynamic and evolving landscape of healthcare entrepreneurship, uncovering how entrepreneurs are leveraging digital innovations to shape the future of healthcare for the benefit of individuals and communities.

7

Healthcare Entrepreneurship and Ethical Considerations

Introduction

As healthcare entrepreneurship continues to evolve, it encounters a range of ethical considerations that need to be carefully navigated. In this chapter, we explore the ethical dimensions of healthcare entrepreneurship, focusing on topics such as patient privacy, data security, informed consent, responsible innovation, and equitable access to healthcare innovations. We will examine the critical role that ethics plays in shaping the development, deployment, and impact of healthcare innovations.

Section 1: Patient Privacy and Data Security

1.1 Data Privacy Concerns

The collection and use of sensitive patient data raise important ethical questions regarding privacy and data security. We will explore the challenges and ethical dilemmas associated with patient data in healthcare entrepreneurship.

1.2 Ethical Data Practices

Entrepreneurs in healthcare must adopt ethical data practices, including secure storage, consent protocols, and transparent data usage, to ensure patient trust and regulatory compliance.

Section 2: Informed Consent and Patient Autonomy

2.1 Informed Decision-Making

Informed consent is a cornerstone of ethical healthcare practice. Entrepreneurs must prioritize clear and transparent communication with patients to respect their autonomy in decision-making.

2.2 Ethical Innovations

Developing healthcare innovations that prioritize patient autonomy and informed consent is critical. We will examine examples of startups and entrepreneurs that have adopted these ethical principles.

Section 3: Responsible Innovation

3.1 Ethical Technology Development

Healthcare entrepreneurs must consider the potential social, ethical, and environmental consequences of their innovations. We will explore the concept of responsible innovation and its role in healthcare entrepreneurship.

3.2 Case Studies: Responsible Innovators

Case studies will highlight entrepreneurs who have integrated ethical considerations into their innovations, demonstrating a commitment to the well-being of both individuals and society.

Section 4: Equitable Access to Healthcare Innovations

4.1 Addressing Healthcare Disparities

Entrepreneurs in healthcare must confront the ethical challenge of ensuring that their innovations do not exacerbate existing healthcare disparities. This section will discuss strategies to promote equitable access.

4.2 Global Health Equity

The quest for global health equity presents ethical considerations related to access, affordability, and the adaptation of innovations to diverse cultural contexts. We will examine initiatives that address these challenges.

Conclusion

Chapter 7 has highlighted the ethical considerations that are integral to healthcare entrepreneurship. As healthcare innovation continues to advance, entrepreneurs must prioritize ethical principles to ensure that their innovations respect patient privacy, prioritize informed consent, foster responsible development, and promote equitable access. By addressing these ethical challenges, healthcare entrepreneurs can build trust with patients, regulators, and the broader healthcare community, ultimately contributing to the betterment of lives in a responsible and sustainable manner. In the subsequent chapters, we will continue to explore the multifaceted and ever-evolving world of healthcare entrepreneurship, shedding light on how entrepreneurs are shaping the future of healthcare while upholding ethical standards.

8

Financing Healthcare Entrepreneurship

Introduction

The success of healthcare entrepreneurship often hinges on securing adequate funding to drive innovation, research, development, and market expansion. In this chapter, we delve into the critical aspect of financing healthcare entrepreneurship, examining the various sources of funding, strategies for securing investment, and the unique challenges faced by healthcare startups. Entrepreneurs must navigate a complex landscape of financing options to bring their healthcare innovations to life.

Section 1: Sources of Funding

1.1 Bootstrapping

Many healthcare entrepreneurs start by self-funding their ventures, using personal savings or earnings from previous projects to kickstart their initiatives. We will explore the advantages and limitations of bootstrapping in healthcare.

1.2 Angel Investors

Angel investors provide early-stage funding to healthcare startups in exchange for equity. We will discuss how angel investments work and their significance in the healthcare entrepreneurship ecosystem.

Section 2: Venture Capital

2.1 The Role of Venture Capital

Venture capital plays a crucial role in healthcare entrepreneurship by providing substantial funding for innovative startups. This section will examine the process of securing venture capital and the unique considerations for healthcare ventures.

2.2 Healthtech and Biotech Investment

We will explore how venture capital firms specialize in healthtech and biotech, focusing on startups that bring disruptive healthcare innovations to the market.

Section 3: Grants and Government Funding

3.1 Grants for Healthcare Innovation

Government agencies and foundations offer grants to support healthcare innovation and research. This section will provide insights into the grant application process and successful case studies.

3.2 Public-Private Partnerships

Public-private partnerships in healthcare innovation can offer financial support, research collaboration, and regulatory guidance. We will discuss the advantages and challenges of such partnerships.

Section 4: Crowdfunding and Digital Platforms

4.1 Crowdfunding in Healthcare

Crowdfunding platforms, such as Kickstarter and Indiegogo, have become viable options for healthcare startups to raise capital. We will examine the use of crowdfunding for healthcare innovations.

4.2 Online Investment Communities

Online platforms like MedStartr and Healthfundr specialize in connecting healthcare startups with investors who have a particular interest in the sector.

Section 5: Challenges in Healthcare Entrepreneurship Financing

5.1 Regulatory Hurdles

Navigating the complex and evolving healthcare regulatory landscape can be a significant challenge for entrepreneurs seeking investment.

5.2 Clinical Validation Costs

Healthcare startups often face substantial expenses related to clinical trials and studies, which can affect their financial planning and ability to secure funding.

Conclusion

Chapter 8 has illuminated the importance of financing in healthcare entrepreneurship. Access to adequate funding is crucial for the development and commercialization of innovative healthcare solutions. Entrepreneurs must carefully consider the sources of funding, align their strategies with their venture's stage and goals, and navigate the unique challenges presented by the healthcare sector's regulatory complexities and clinical validation requirements. In the upcoming chapters, we will continue to explore the multifaceted and ever-evolving world of healthcare entrepreneurship, shedding light on the diverse ways in which entrepreneurs are shaping the future of healthcare by securing the necessary financial resources.

9

Scaling Healthcare Entrepreneurship

Introduction

Scaling healthcare entrepreneurship is a pivotal phase in the journey of healthcare startups. This chapter delves into the challenges, strategies, and considerations involved in taking healthcare innovations from initial concepts to widespread impact. We will explore the diverse pathways to scaling healthcare entrepreneurship, including expanding to new markets, partnerships, and achieving regulatory compliance.

Section 1: The Path to Scale

1.1 Scaling Strategies

We will examine the key strategies and approaches that healthcare entrepreneurs can employ to scale their ventures, from market expansion to diversification and product enhancement.

1.2 Overcoming Growth Challenges

Entrepreneurs must navigate a variety of challenges, including resource limitations, competition, and regulatory hurdles. We will discuss how these challenges can be addressed in the scaling process.

Section 2: Market Expansion

2.1 Expanding Geographically

Healthcare entrepreneurs often explore opportunities for geographic expansion, whether within a country or internationally. This section will discuss the considerations and strategies for scaling into new markets.

2.2 Niche Markets

Entrepreneurs can also identify and target niche markets within the healthcare sector, catering to specific needs and demographics. We will explore examples of successful niche market scaling.

Section 3: Strategic Partnerships and Collaborations

3.1 Leveraging Partnerships

Collaborations with healthcare providers, insurers, pharmaceutical companies, and other stakeholders can significantly aid in scaling healthcare entrepreneurship. We will examine the role of partnerships in achieving scale.

3.2 Case Studies: Successful Collaborations

Case studies will showcase healthcare startups that have successfully leveraged strategic partnerships to expand their reach and impact.

Section 4: Regulatory Compliance and Quality Assurance

4.1 Regulatory Challenges

Achieving and maintaining regulatory compliance is a critical aspect of scaling healthcare entrepreneurship. We will discuss the unique regulatory challenges faced by healthcare startups.

4.2 Ensuring Quality and Safety

Scaling healthcare ventures requires a focus on quality assurance and patient safety. We will explore how entrepreneurs ensure that their innovations maintain high standards as they grow.

Conclusion

Chapter 9 has shed light on the complex and dynamic process of scaling healthcare entrepreneurship. Entrepreneurs in healthcare face a myriad of challenges as they strive to expand their reach and impact. By carefully considering strategies for market expansion, forming strategic partnerships, and addressing regulatory compliance and quality assurance, healthcare startups can navigate the scaling process successfully. In the subsequent chapters, we will continue to explore the multifaceted and ever-evolving world of healthcare entrepreneurship, unveiling how entrepreneurs are shaping the future of healthcare by achieving scale and broader impact.

10

Healthcare Entrepreneurship and Future Trends

Introduction

The landscape of healthcare entrepreneurship is continuously evolving, driven by technological advancements, shifting demographics, and changing healthcare needs. In this chapter, we explore the future trends and emerging opportunities in healthcare entrepreneurship. We will delve into the potential impact of artificial intelligence, telemedicine, personalized medicine, and other innovative developments, as well as the changing regulatory and ethical considerations that entrepreneurs must navigate in this dynamic field.

Section 1: Artificial Intelligence and Machine Learning

1.1 AI-Driven Diagnostics and Treatment

The role of artificial intelligence and machine learning in healthcare is expanding rapidly. We will examine the potential for AI to revolutionize diagnostics, treatment recommendations, and drug discovery.

1.2 Ethical AI Use

As AI plays a more prominent role in healthcare, ethical considerations surrounding data privacy, transparency, and bias must be addressed. We will discuss the ethical dimensions of AI in healthcare entrepreneurship.

Section 2: Telemedicine and Virtual Care

2.1 Remote Healthcare Delivery

Telemedicine and virtual care are expected to continue to grow, improving access to healthcare and patient experiences. We will explore the future of telemedicine and the entrepreneurial opportunities it presents.

2.2 Regulatory Changes

The regulatory landscape for telemedicine is evolving. We will discuss the potential impact of regulatory changes on healthcare entrepreneurship in this sector.

Section 3: Personalized and Precision Medicine

3.1 Genomic Sequencing and Precision Medicine

Genomic sequencing and personalized medicine will play an increasingly prominent role in healthcare. We will explore how healthcare entrepreneurs can leverage this trend.

3.2 Ethical Considerations in Genomics

As genomic data becomes more integrated into healthcare, ethical considerations related to data privacy, consent, and equity are crucial. We will delve into these ethical challenges.

Section 4: Value-Based Care and Population Health

4.1 Shifting Toward Value-Based Care

Healthcare is moving from a fee-for-service model to a value-based care approach, emphasizing patient outcomes. We will discuss the opportunities and challenges for healthcare entrepreneurs in this shift.

4.2 Population Health Management

Entrepreneurs are playing a key role in developing innovative solutions for population health management, focusing on preventive care and better health outcomes for communities.

Conclusion

Chapter 10 has provided insights into the future trends of healthcare entrepreneurship. As healthcare continues to evolve, entrepreneurs will have the opportunity to shape the industry by leveraging artificial intelligence, telemedicine, personalized medicine, and other emerging trends. However, they must also consider the changing regulatory and ethical landscape in their pursuit of innovative solutions. In the following chapters, we will continue to explore the multifaceted and ever-evolving world of healthcare entrepreneurship, unveiling how entrepreneurs are shaping the future of healthcare for the betterment of individuals and communities.

11

Healthcare Entrepreneurship and Resilience

Introduction

Resilience is a critical attribute for healthcare entrepreneurs. This chapter explores the concept of resilience in the context of healthcare entrepreneurship. We will delve into the challenges that entrepreneurs face, the importance of adaptability, and strategies for building resilience in the ever-evolving healthcare landscape. Resilient entrepreneurs are better equipped to navigate setbacks, overcome obstacles, and drive meaningful change in the healthcare sector.

Section 1: Challenges in Healthcare Entrepreneurship

1.1 Regulatory Hurdles

The complex and evolving regulatory environment in healthcare can present significant challenges for entrepreneurs. We will explore the difficulties entrepreneurs encounter and the importance of resilience in addressing them.

1.2 Clinical Validation and Research

The rigorous clinical validation required in healthcare can be time-consuming and expensive. Entrepreneurs must exhibit resilience in navigating the demands of research and development.

Section 2: Adaptability and Learning

2.1 The Need for Adaptability

Adaptability is a core trait of resilient healthcare entrepreneurs. We will discuss the importance of staying flexible in response to changing market dynamics, technology, and patient needs.

2.2 Continuous Learning

Entrepreneurs must engage in continuous learning to remain competitive. We will explore how embracing lifelong learning can contribute to resilience and success.

Section 3: Coping with Failure

3.1 Overcoming Setbacks

Setbacks and failures are an inevitable part of entrepreneurship. Resilient entrepreneurs have the ability to bounce back from disappointments and view failures as opportunities for growth.

3.2 Case Studies: Resilient Entrepreneurs

Case studies of entrepreneurs who faced adversity and emerged stronger will illustrate the importance of resilience in healthcare entrepreneurship.

Section 4: Building a Support Network

4.1 Mentorship and Peer Support

Having a network of mentors and peers can provide invaluable support and guidance. We will discuss how such relationships can bolster resilience.

4.2 Mental Health and Well-Being

The mental health and well-being of healthcare entrepreneurs are integral to their resilience. We will explore strategies for maintaining mental and emotional health.

Conclusion

Chapter 11 has emphasized the importance of resilience in healthcare entrepreneurship. The ability to adapt to challenges, learn continuously, cope with failure, and build a support network is crucial for entrepreneurs striving to make a positive impact in the healthcare sector. By developing resilience, healthcare entrepreneurs can navigate the complexities of the industry and drive meaningful change that benefits individuals and communities. In the upcoming chapters, we will continue to explore the multifaceted and ever-evolving world of healthcare entrepreneurship, shedding light on how entrepreneurs are shaping the future of healthcare while embodying the attributes of resilience.

12

Healthcare Entrepreneurship and Social Responsibility

Introduction

In the healthcare sector, social responsibility takes on a paramount role. This chapter explores the concept of social responsibility in healthcare entrepreneurship. We will delve into the ethical, environmental, and community-focused dimensions of social responsibility, emphasizing the importance of contributing positively to society and addressing pressing global health issues.

Section 1: Ethical Business Practices

1.1 Ethical Leadership

Entrepreneurs in healthcare must lead with ethical principles, ensuring that their business practices prioritize patient well-being, data privacy, and transparency.

1.2 Responsible Marketing

The way healthcare innovations are marketed and promoted plays a crucial role in social responsibility. We will discuss the ethical considerations in healthcare marketing.

Section 2: Environmental Sustainability

2.1 Reducing Environmental Impact

The healthcare sector has a significant environmental footprint. Entrepreneurs can contribute to sustainability by minimizing waste, energy consumption, and the carbon footprint of healthcare operations.

2.2 Case Studies: Sustainable Healthcare Initiatives

Case studies will showcase healthcare startups that have implemented sustainable practices, reducing their environmental impact.

Section 3: Community Engagement and Impact

3.1 Community Health Initiatives

Socially responsible healthcare entrepreneurs engage with and invest in local communities, addressing health disparities and improving community well-being.

3.2 Global Health Initiatives

Entrepreneurs with a global perspective can contribute to global health through initiatives that address healthcare disparities, access, and disease prevention.

Section 4: Philanthropy and Giving Back

4.1 Philanthropic Endeavors

Giving back to society is a core component of social responsibility. We will explore the philanthropic efforts of healthcare entrepreneurs.

4.2 Healthcare Access for Underserved Communities

Entrepreneurs can contribute to social responsibility by focusing on initiatives that provide healthcare access to underserved and marginalized communities.

Conclusion

Chapter 12 has emphasized the importance of social responsibility in healthcare entrepreneurship. Entrepreneurs in the healthcare sector have a unique opportunity to make a positive impact on individuals, communities, and the environment. By embracing ethical business practices, environmental sustainability, community engagement, and philanthropy, healthcare entrepreneurs can contribute to a more socially responsible healthcare industry, ultimately benefiting the well-being of people and the planet. In the subsequent chapters, we will continue to explore the multifaceted and ever-evolving world of healthcare entrepreneurship, unveiling how entrepreneurs are shaping the future of healthcare with a strong commitment to social responsibility.

13

Summary

The chapters provided a comprehensive exploration of healthcare entrepreneurship, covering various aspects of this dynamic field. Here is a summary of the key points discussed in each chapter:

Chapter 1: "Entrepreneurship in Healthcare: Innovations for Better Lives"
- Introduced the concept of healthcare entrepreneurship and its impact on improving healthcare delivery.
- Explored the role of entrepreneurship in driving innovation and addressing healthcare challenges.
- Discussed the potential for entrepreneurs to shape the future of healthcare and enhance the quality of life.

Chapter 2: "Technological Advancements in Healthcare Entrepreneurship"
- Examined the impact of technology on healthcare entrepreneurship, with a focus on telemedicine, wearable health tech, and AI applications.
- Showcased examples of startups and entrepreneurs using technology to revolutionize healthcare delivery and enhance patient outcomes.

Chapter 3: "Biotechnology and Healthcare Entrepreneurship"
- Explored the significance of biotechnology in healthcare entrepreneurship, with a focus on precision medicine, cell and gene therapies, and drug

development.

- Discussed the challenges and opportunities faced by biotech startups in the healthcare sector.

Chapter 4: "Social Entrepreneurship in Healthcare"
- Highlighted the role of social entrepreneurship in addressing healthcare access, equity, and sustainability.
- Discussed the importance of addressing social determinants of health and improving healthcare outcomes for underserved communities.

Chapter 5: "Global Healthcare Entrepreneurship and Impact"
- Explored the global landscape of healthcare entrepreneurship and the role of cross-border collaboration and global health initiatives.
- Showcased examples of entrepreneurs making a positive impact on healthcare access and equity worldwide.

Chapter 6: "Healthcare Entrepreneurship in the Digital Age"
- Examined the impact of digital innovations on healthcare entrepreneurship, including EHRs, telemedicine, AI, and patient-centric care.
- Discussed the importance of ethical considerations in the digital age of healthcare entrepreneurship.

Chapter 7: "Healthcare Entrepreneurship and Ethical Considerations"
- Explored ethical dimensions in healthcare entrepreneurship, including patient privacy, data security, informed consent, responsible innovation, and equitable access.
- Discussed the ethical challenges and responsibilities of healthcare entrepreneurs.

Chapter 8: "Financing Healthcare Entrepreneurship"
- Emphasized the importance of securing adequate funding for healthcare entrepreneurship, including sources such as bootstrapping, angel investors, venture capital, and grants.

- Explored the unique challenges related to financing healthcare startups.

Chapter 9: "Scaling Healthcare Entrepreneurship"
 - Examined the strategies and challenges involved in scaling healthcare entrepreneurship, including market expansion, partnerships, and regulatory compliance.
 - Discussed the changing healthcare landscape and opportunities for entrepreneurs to achieve scale.

Chapter 10: "Healthcare Entrepreneurship and Future Trends"
 - Explored emerging trends in healthcare entrepreneurship, including AI, telemedicine, personalized medicine, value-based care, and population health.
 - Discussed the ethical and regulatory considerations associated with these trends.

Chapter 11: "Healthcare Entrepreneurship and Resilience"
 - Highlighted the importance of resilience in healthcare entrepreneurship, with a focus on addressing challenges, adapting to change, coping with failure, and building a support network.
 - Showcased case studies of resilient entrepreneurs who overcame adversity.

Chapter 12: "Healthcare Entrepreneurship and Social Responsibility"
 - Explored the concept of social responsibility in healthcare entrepreneurship, covering ethical business practices, environmental sustainability, community engagement, and philanthropy.
 - Discussed the role of socially responsible healthcare entrepreneurs in contributing positively to society and the environment.

These chapters collectively offer a comprehensive overview of the multifaceted and ever-evolving world of healthcare entrepreneurship. Entrepreneurs in this field play a vital role in shaping the future of healthcare, with a strong commitment to innovation, ethics, and social responsibility.

www.ingramcontent.com/pod-product-compliance
Lightning Source LLC
LaVergne TN
LVHW012131070526
838202LV00056B/5944